Trusting and Believing God

Righteousness by Faith

*by **Rick Streight***

Second Edition

"And I will give them an heart to know me, that I am the LORD: and they shall be my people, and I will be their God: for they shall return unto me with their whole heart" (Jeremiah 24:7).

Falling in Love with God & Our Fellow Man

A Blueprint for Translation

Published by
TEACH Services, Inc.
www.TEACHServices.com

Copyright © 2011 Rick Streight.
ISBN-13: 978-157258- 673-4
Library of Congress Control Number: 2011923671

Published by
TEACH Services, Inc.
www.TEACHServices.com

Dedication

To God's Remnant People, like myself, who want a better understanding of what it means to be a Christian fighting the good fight of faith and hastening Jesus' Second Coming.

"For Zion's sake will I not hold my peace (silence), and for Jerusalem's sake I will not rest until the righteousness there of go forth as brightness, and the salvation there of as a lamp that burneth."

"And the Gentiles shall see thy righteousness, and all the Kings thy glory: and thou shalt be called by a new name, which the mouth of the Lord shall name."

"And give him no rest, till he establish, and till he make Jerusalem a praise in the earth." (Isaiah 62: 1, 2, 7)

In light of the Cross of Calvary we must tell others about Jesus, we must encourage and strengthen one another in the faith. We must be "Living Epistles" correctly representing Christianity to the world.

Pray for me, I'll be praying for you!

"I BESEECH you therefore brethren, by the mercies of God, that ye present your bodies a living sacrifice, holy, acceptable unto God, which is your reasonable service." (Romans 12:1)

Table of Contents

All Scripture in this study is from the King James Version Bible, unless otherwise noted.

Acknowledgments

There have been many influences that led me to write this book. Reading God's Word with a heartfelt desire to know Jesus better, things I learned were so precious to me I wrote them down, then the Holy Spirit convicted me to share what I had learned with others.

I thank my dear wife, Theresa, for being faithful and patient with me, giving me good advice, helping me spell words correctly and spending many long hours on the computer putting the rough copy together for me to submit to TEACH Services, Inc.

I was not a Christian yet, but when I joined the U.S. Navy and went to Military War Time Boot Camp, I learned, 'Not my will, but U.S. Government's Will be done!' As a Christian I understood more about what it means, 'Not my will, but God's Will be done!"

When I went to an Amazing Facts Crusade, Evangelist Joe Crews faithfully taught me how to study the Bible. He showed me the difference between the Perverted Gospel (salvation in sin) and the Genuine Gospel (salvation from sin.) He also showed me an appreciation of the writings of Ellen G. White.

And finally, I want to acknowledge the faithfulness of 'those Cloud of Witnesses' in Hebrews the 11th chapter who would rather die than sin against God. They taught me to have a strong Spiritual Backbone, even if the Truth is not popular.

Trusting and Believing God

Righteousness by Faith

by Rick and Theresa Streight

It is my spiritual good pleasure to share with you, the reader, the journey that has changed my life and can change yours as well! Not only a good life but 'the abundant life.' Not only the abundant life but eternal life!

"I will instruct thee and teach thee in the ways which thou shalt go." (Psalm 32: 8)

Our Personal Testimony

Twenty-five years ago, my wife, Theresa, and I made a decision to accept Jesus Christ as our personal Lord and Savior from sin. The Bible's proclamation that Jesus would save people from their sins had been manifested in our lives: "And she shall bring forth a son, and thou shalt call his name JESUS: for he shall save his people from their sins" (Matthew 1:21).

We studied God's Word, prayed, and experienced *much needed* chastisement from the Lord. God's Word is so true! Reading in James 1:2-4, we understood the important role trials play in our lives, maturing our characters: "My brethren, count it all joy when ye fall into divers temptations; knowing this, that the trying of your faith worketh patience. But let patience have her perfect work, that ye may be perfect [mature] and entire, wanting nothing." We knew that we needed God to work in our lives, and He did. Deuteronomy 8:16 comes to mind as I think about our experience: "that he [God] might humble thee, and that he might prove thee, to do thee good at thy latter end." (I recommend that you read *Thoughts from the Mount of Blessing*, pp. 29-31, to gain a deeper understanding of the Christian walk.)

Looking back at our first six years as newborns in Christ, we remember the peace and joy of knowing that we were sons and daughters of God. (Read John 1:12, 13.) Unfortunately, from time to time we would be careless in our devotional life. Since we were not mature Christians, we would find ourselves unable to resist temptation and would sin against God. This was a frustrating experience because in our hearts we loved God and wanted to do His will. We wanted to be a good witness, but we failed many times. We know of other Christians who have had that same experience.

Dear reader, could you be one of them? Don't stop reading; there is encouragement coming! In the Bible,

God records a similar experience that Paul had in Romans 7:14-24. In verse 14, Paul admits that he is "carnal, sold under sin." Paul goes on to lament in verse 15 regarding his behavior: "For that which I do I allow not: for what I would, that do I not; but what I hate, that do I." In verse 24, Paul poses a question about the deliverance from sin: "O wretched man that I am! who shall deliver me from the body of this death?"

In the next chapter, Paul writes, "For to be carnally minded is death; but to be spiritually minded is life and peace" (Romans 8:6). Ellen White tells us this was Paul's unconverted experience. (Read *Christ's Object Lessons*, p. 201; *Steps to Christ*, pp. 19, 20, 37, 38; and Testimonies for the Church Volume 1, pp. 161, 162.)

Quoting from a personal letter from the late evangelist Joe Crews regarding Romans 7, he writes these thoughts: "Paul is describing the role of the law in bringing a person to Christ. He is also describing the experience of an individual who has been convicted and enlightened by the law but who has not yet laid hold of the grace of Christ for salvation."

Paul was *convicted,* but not *converted* (born again). Then Paul had a deeper experience: "I thank God through Jesus Christ our Lord. So then with my mind I myself serve the law of God; but with the flesh the law of sin" (Romans 7:25).

Paul found the secret key that unlocked his up-and-down experience of bondage and rejoiced in his new experience. He found liberty in Christ Jesus. The whole eighth chapter of Romans explains the born again power of liberty, grace, and consistent, victorious Christian living to God's glory. What an encouragement to all of us!

Leaving Paul's experience and coming back to ours, God worked a miracle when we felt our need to pray for answers. We dug deeper into God's Word. One morning as we were studying Luke 6:46-49, dealing with the man who built his house upon the Rock, we asked for more wisdom from our heavenly Counselor, the Holy Spirit. I had read in Hebrews 12:1, 2 about the "cloud of witnesses" who would rather die than sin against God. (For your additional encouragement, please read Hebrews 11.) God wants us to part from all besetting sins and realize that Jesus is "not only the Author, but also the Finisher of our faith." (Hebrews 12:2)

From reading this study, *Trusting and Believing God*, it is our hope that we will all feel our need to draw closer to Jesus and have more of a willingness to die to self. This is the covenant we made with God when we were baptized:

"Know ye not, that so many of us as were baptized into Jesus Christ were baptized into his death? Therefore we are buried with him by baptism into death: that like as Christ was raised up from the dead by the glory of the Father, even so we also should walk in newness of life. . . . But now being made free from sin, and become servants to God, ye have your fruit unto holiness, and the end everlasting life" (Romans 6:3, 4, 22).

Ellen White wrote the following in her book *Sons and Daughters of God*: "Let no one say, 'I cannot overcome my defects of character'; for if this is your decision, then you cannot have eternal life. The impossibility is all in your will. If you *will not*, that constitutes the *cannot*. The real difficulty is the corruption of an unsanctified heart, and an unwillingness to submit to the will of God" (p. 115).

The Lord had answered our prayers. Our doubts were gone, and now we wanted to shout to the world and encourage others to abide in Christ, trust and believe God, and experience righteousness by faith. This marked the beginning of a new phase in our life of witnessing and encouraging.

God is sealing (maturing) His people. This is what the Spirit of Prophecy and John the Revelator have to say:

"(Revelation 7:2.) Seal Is a Settling Into Truth.— Just as soon as the people of God are sealed in their foreheads—it is not any seal or mark that can be seen, but a settling into the truth, both intellectually and spiritually, so they cannot be moved" (*S.D.A. Bible Commentary*, vol. 4, p. 1161).

"The seal of the living God will be placed upon those only who bear a likeness to Christ in character. . . . Let us strive with all power that God has given us to be among the hundred and forty-four thousand" (*S.D.A. Bible Commentary*, vol. 7, p. 970).

"And I looked, and, lo, a Lamb stood on the mount Sion, and with him an hundred forty and four thousand, having his Father's name written in their foreheads. These are they which follow the Lamb withersoever he goeth" (Revelation 14:1, 4).

"And grieve not the holy Spirit of God, whereby ye are sealed unto the day of redemption" (Ephesians 4:30).

May Paul's experience of true conversion be our own. Read Paul's own words as recorded by Luke: "And herein do I exercise myself, to have always a conscience void of offence toward God, and toward men" (Acts 24:16).

And the Spirit bears witness as Peter, also, has the same type of conviction: "The like figure whereunto even baptism doth also now save us (not the putting away of the filth of the flesh, but the answer of a good conscience toward God,) by the resurrection of Jesus" (1 Peter 3:21).

The question is, how can a true believer (God knows who is and who isn't) continue in sin after knowing the price Jesus paid to have our sins forgiven? WARNING: "For if we sin wilfully after that we have received the knowledge of the truth, there remaineth no more sacrifice for sins" (Hebrews10:26). Also, "For if after they have escaped the pollutions of the world through the knowledge of the Lord and Savior Jesus Christ, they are again entangled therein, and overcome, the latter end is worse with them than the beginning. For it had been better for them not to have known the way of righteousness, than, after they have known it, to turn from the holy commandment delivered unto them" (2 Peter 2:20, 21).

"In this the children of God are manifest and the children of the devil . . ." (1 John 3:10)

"He that committeth sin is of the devil . . . For this purpose the Son of God was manifested, that he might destroy the works of the devil." (1 John 3:8)

God can give us the power we need to keep sin out of our lives. He gives us the following promises: "I can do all things through Christ which strengtheneth me" (Philippians 4:13). In 1 Corinthians 10:13, we read, "There hath no temptation taken you such as is common to man: but God is faithful, who will not suffer you to be tempted above that ye are able; but will with the temptation also make a way to escape, that ye may be able to bear it."

The Bible tells us that the truth will make us free (John 8:32). Paul encourages us to walk with Christ: "There is therefore now no condemnation to them which are in Christ Jesus, who walk not after the flesh, but after the Spirit. Nay, in all these things we are more than conquerors through him that loved us" (Romans 8:1, 37).

So how do we show our love to God? The Bible tells us that if we love God we will keep His commandments (John 14:15). In 1 John 5:2-4, the idea of keeping God's commandments is expanded upon: "By this we know that we love the children of God, when we love God, and keep his commandments. For this is the love of God, that we keep his commandments: and his commandments are not grievous. For whatsoever is born of God overcometh the world: and this is the victory that overcometh the world, even our faith."

Even with these promises, many Christians doubt that they can overcome. Do we really believe God's Word when it says that with Christ in us we are stronger than Satan? Read 1 John 5:18 as a reminder of this promise: "We know that whosoever is born of God sinneth not; but he that is begotten of God keepeth himself, and that wicked one toucheth him not."

If we want to love God and love others as Jesus did

(Matthew 22:36-40), then we must take inventory of our lives and spend more time with Him. By beholding Christ, we become more like Him. Here is what the apostle Paul says: "Now the Lord is that Spirit: and where the Spirit of the Lord is, there is liberty. But we all, with open face beholding as in a glass the glory of the Lord, are changed into the same image from glory to glory, even as by the Spirit of the Lord" (2 Corinthians 3:17, 18). If we follow God, we will emulate Christ's actions. "He that saith he abideth in him ought himself also so to walk, even as he walked" (1 John 2:6).

Jesus is our example in all areas of life. In 1 Peter 2:21-25, we read what Peter has to say about Christ's example: "For even hereunto were ye called: because Christ also suffered for us, leaving us an example, that ye should follow his steps: Who did no sin, neither was guile found in his mouth: Who, when he was reviled, reviled not again; when he suffered, he threatened not; but committed himself to him that judgeth righteously: Who his own self bare our sins in his own body on the tree, that we, being dead to sins, should live unto righteousness: by whose stripes ye were healed. For ye were [past tense] as sheep going astray; but are now returned unto the Shepherd and Bishop of your souls."

Because Jesus' mother was Mary, He was human. Because Jesus' Father was God, He was divine. We, as Christians, know only too well how human we are, but it is encouraging to remember that we also realize as sons and daughters of God—we have put on the divine nature. Peter again explains: "According as his divine power hath given unto us all things that pertain unto life and godliness, through the knowledge of him that hath called us to glory and virtue: Whereby are given unto us exceeding great and precious promises: that by these ye might be partakers of the divine nature having escaped the corruption that is in the world through lust" (2 Peter 1:3, 4).

Earlier in the New Testament, John wrote the following about our heavenly Father: "But as many as received him, to them gave he power to become the sons [and daughters] of God, even to them that believe on his name: Which were born, not of blood, nor of the will of the flesh, nor of the will of man, but of God" (John 1:12, 13).

Through Christ, we become a new creation. "Therefore if any man be in Christ, he is a new creature: old things are passed away; behold, all things are become new" (1 Corinthians 5:17). As we deepen our relationship, we grow further in Him, which John writes about in 1 John 3:9: " Whosoever is born of God doth not commit sin; for his seed remaineth in him: and he cannot sin, because he is born of God."

As Seventh-day Adventists, we believe God's Word is powerful—it can create and recreate us. When we accept Jesus as our Lord and Savior, we receive imputed righteousness, which we call justification. We also experience by faith, imparted righteousness, which we call

sanctification. Sanctification means that the righteousness becomes a reality; we are made righteous.
Sanctification grows as our knowledge of God's Word
increases.

Ellen White makes an interesting statement regarding Jesus' ministry on earth: "The Savior took upon
Himself the infirmities of humanity and lived a sinless
life, that men might have no fear that because of the
weakness of human nature they could not overcome.
Christ came to make us 'partakers of the divine nature,'
and His life declares that humanity combined with di-
vinity, does not commit sin" (*The Ministry of Healing,*
p. 180).

Praise God that we have a solid foundation!
"Nevertheless the foundation of God standeth sure, having this seal, The Lord knoweth them that are his. And,
let every one that nameth the name of Christ depart from
iniquity" (2 Timothy 2:19). (Read also *Testimonies for
the Church*, vol. 5, p. 49.)

As we build our foundation on Christ, we must guard
against temptation. "Little children, let no man deceive
you: he that doeth righteousness is righteous, even as he
is righteous" (1 John 3:7). Peter also adds his warning to
that of John: "Forasmuch then as Christ hath suffered
for us in the flesh, arm yourselves likewise with the
same mind: for he that hath suffered in the flesh hath
ceased from sin; That he no longer should live the rest of
his time in the flesh to the lusts of men, but to the will of
God" (1 Peter 4:1, 2).

Abiding in Christ

By abiding in Christ—"which is Christ in you, the hope of glory" (Colossians 1:27)—we are keenly aware of God's presence in our lives at all times. If we believed in our heart that Jesus is with us every moment of every day, there would be things we would do and things we wouldn't do. For example, can we really call ourselves Christians if we are in open rebellion to God's will in our lives? Any compromise of truth dishonors Jesus through misrepresentation.

One of God's ten commandments tells us that "thou shalt not take the name of the LORD thy God in vain; for the LORD will not hold him guiltless that taketh his name in vain" (Exodus 20:7). King Solomon understood this principle: "Remove far from me vanity and lies: give me neither poverty nor riches; feed me with food convenient for me: Lest I be full, and deny thee, and say, Who is the LORD? or lest I be poor, and steal, and take the name of my God in vain" (Proverbs 30:8, 9).

From reading the above scriptures we conclude that calling yourself a Christian and not acting like one is like taking the Lord's name in vain. If we want to live as a dedicated Christian, we will live "by every word that proceedeth out of the mouth of God" (Matthew 4:4).

Ellen White provided counsel regarding the conduct of Christians and their connection with Christ.

"Profession was worthless. If their life and character were not in harmony with God's law, they were not His people" (*The Desire of Ages,* p. 107).

"It should be understood whether they are simply taking the name of Seventh-Day Adventists, or whether they are taking their stand on the Lord's side, to come out from the world and be separate, and touch not the unclean thing" (*Testimonies for the Church,* vol. 6, p. 95).

"There is an election of individuals and a people, the only election found in the word of God, where man is elected to be saved. Many have looked at the end, thinking they were surely elected to have heavenly bliss; but this is not the election the Bible reveals. Man is elected to work out his own salvation with fear and trembling. He is elected to put on the armor, to fight the good fight of faith. He is elected to use the means God has placed within his reach to war against every unholy lust, while Satan is playing the game of life for his soul. He is elected to watch unto prayer, to search the Scriptures, and to avoid entering into temptation. He is elected to have faith continually. He is elected to be obedient to every word that proceedeth out of the mouth of God, and that he may be, not a hearer only, but a doer of the word. This is Bible election" (*Testimonies to Ministers and Gospel Workers*, pp. 453, 454).

We know we need physical food to survive physically. But if we want to deepen our Christian experience, we need spiritual food every day to survive spiritually.

Throughout Scripture God instructs us to store His Word in our hearts and live it in our lives. He will tell us things we should do and things we shouldn't do. When we obey His voice, which speaks to us, we know we are living in the Spirit and not according to the flesh. (Read Romans 8:1 and Galatians 6:7, 8.)

As we are navigating our Christian walk, we can turn to the book of James for practical Christian advice. We read: "Wherefore lay apart all filthiness and superfluity of naughtiness, and receive with meekness the engrafted word, which is able to save your souls. But be ye doers of the word, and not hearers only, deceiving your own selves" (James 1:21, 22).

We are to be so intimately connected to God's Word that we live according to its precepts. If we are not "doers of the word," then our Christianity is not genuine.

Trusting and Believing God

God wants us to trust and believe in Him from the heart. Once we exhibit this behavior, we are bearing fruit. In Acts 8:37, the story is told of the eunuch who believed and sought baptism: "And Philip said, If thou believest with all thine heart, thou mayest. And he answered and said, I believe that Jesus Christ is the Son of God." King David also spoke about the importance of believing in God and speaking the truth: " Lord, who shall abide in thy tabernacle? who shall dwell in thy holy hill? He that walketh uprightly, and worketh righteousness, and speaketh the truth in his heart" (Psalm 15:1, 2).

Spiritual fruit will be evident in our lives through the act of forgiveness and mercy to our fellow man and love for God by keeping His commandments: "And hereby we do know that we know him, if we keep his commandments. He that saith, I know him, and keepeth not his commandments, is a liar, and the truth is not in him" (1 John 2:3, 4).

Revelation 14:12 confirms what outward fruit we will bear if we are a true follower of Christ: "Here is the patience of the saints: here are they that keep the commandments of God, and the faith of Jesus.

The World's Greatest Need—A True Witness

"The world needs a practical demonstration of what the grace of God can do in restoring to human beings their lost kingship, giving them mastery of themselves. There is nothing that the world needs so much as a knowledge of the gospel's saving power revealed in Christlike lives" (*The Ministry of Healing*, pp. 132, 133).

The world needs a Savior, and as Christ's representatives on earth, we have the privilege of sharing the good news with others. The Bible says:

"A little one shall become a thousand, and a small one a strong nation: I the LORD will hasten it in his time" (Isaiah 60:22).

"A true witness delivereth souls: but a deceitful witness speaketh lies" (Proverbs 14:25).

"And this gospel of the kingdom shall be preached in all the world for a witness unto all the nations; and then shall the end come" (Matthew 24:14).

Our actions speak louder than our words! Jesus reveals to us the importance of living the truth: "And for their sakes I sanctify myself, that they also might be sanctified through the truth" (John 17:19).

Like Jesus, may we, as representatives of Him, be strong in His strength and non-compromising in truth that others would also be encouraged to be faithful to God. Fortunately, we do not have to walk alone; we can call on the name of the Lord. "Preserve Me, O God, for in thee do I put my trust" (Psalm 16:1).

May we honestly in our heart ask ourselves: <u>WHAT KIND OF CHURCH WOULD MY CHURCH BE IF EVERYONE WAS JUST LIKE ME?</u>

Ellen White encourages us to submit to God: "A union with Christ by living faith is enduring; every other union must perish. Christ first chose us, paying an infinite price for our redemption; and the true believer chooses Christ as first and last and best in everything. . . . All who form this union must feel their need of the atoning blood of Christ. They must have a change of heart. They must submit their own will to the will of God. There will be a struggle with outward and internal obstacles. There must be a painful work of <u>detachment</u> as well as a work of <u>attachment</u>. Pride, selfishness, vanity, worldliness—sin in all its forms—must be overcome if we would enter into a union with Christ" (*Testimonies for the Church*, vol. 5, p. 231).

The reason why many individuals find the Christian life so hard, why they are so fickle, so variable, is that they try to attach themselves to Christ without first detaching themselves from their cherished idols. Ellen White continues her counsel from the above quote with the following: "After the union with Christ has been formed, it can be preserved only by earnest prayer and untiring effort. We must resist, we must deny, we must conquer self. Through the grace of Christ, by courage, by faith, by watchfulness, we may gain the victory" (Ibid).

Romans 13:14 reminds us of our obligation to put on

Jesus and shun anything that takes us away from Christ: "But put ye on the Lord, Jesus Christ, and make not provision for the flesh, to fulfill the lusts thereof."

In keeping an eternal perspective, may we always remind ourselves that we, as Christians, are different from the world. The Bible says, "Love not the world, neither the things that are in the world" (1 John 2:15). Also, Colossians 3:1, 2 says, "If ye then be risen with Christ, seek those things which are above, where Christ sitteth on the right hand of God. Set your affection on things above, not on things on the earth."

As we look toward heaven, we must beware of distractions and other gods. Our attitude toward the TV should be the same as our association with worldly people. We should seek to do good and not feed the flesh. If Jesus would approve, watch it. If not, then don't. Don't let sports, hobbies, or your job become your god. If we let them, these activities and interests absorb so much time that we forget to keep the armor of God on, staying strong in Jesus.

We must keep fresh in our mind the grace of the cross and the reality that we have been bought with the precious blood of Jesus. We are not our own. "What? Know ye not that your body is the temple of the Holy Ghost which is in you, which ye have of God, and ye are not your own? For ye are bought with a price: therefore glorify God in your body, and in your spirit, which are God's" (1 Corinthians 6:19, 20).

Ellen White wrote, "There is no power in you apart from Christ, but it is your privilege to have Christ abiding in your heart by faith, and He can overcome sin in you, when you cooperate with His efforts. . . . You may be living epistles, known and read of all men. You are not to be a dead letter, but a living one, testifying to the world that Jesus is able to save" (*Our High Calling,* p. 76).

Jesus trusted and believed His Father; He wants us to trust and believe Him. It is easy to see what sin has done to our world and our lives. But more importantly, we must recognize what a great sacrifice Jesus made taking our sins on His own body and experiencing the second death. Please prayerfully study these scriptures:

> "But we see Jesus, who was made a little lower than the angels for the suffering of death, crowned with glory and honour; that he by the grace of God should taste death for every man" (Hebrews 2:9).

> "For God so loved the world, that he gave his only begotten Son, that whosoever believeth in him should not perish, but have everlasting life" (John 3:16).

Ellen White explains why man was shut out from God and the life-saving role Jesus played in restoring our connection with God and defeating the evil one:

"By sin man was shut out from God. Except for the plan of redemption, eternal separation from God, the darkness of unending night, would have been his. Through the Saviour's sacrifice, communion with God is again made possible. We may not in person approach into His presence; in our sin we may not look upon His face; but we can behold Him and commune with Him in Jesus, the Saviour. 'The light of the knowledge of the glory of God,' is revealed 'in the face of Jesus Christ.' God is 'in Christ, reconciling the world unto Himself.' 2 Corinthians 4:6; 5:19.

"And while Christ opens heaven to man, the life which He imparts opens the heart of man to heaven. Sin not only shuts us away from God, but destroys in the human soul both the desire and the capacity for knowing Him. All this work of evil it is Christ's mission to undo. The facilities of the soul, paralyzed by sin, the darkened mind, the perverted will, He has power to invigorate and to restore.

"The result of the eating of the tree of knowledge of good and evil is manifest in every man's experience. There is in his nature a bent to evil, a force which, unaided, he cannot resist. To withstand this force, to attain that ideal which in his inmost soul he accepts as alone worthy, he can find help in but one power. That power is Christ. Co-operation with that power is man's greatest need"(*Education*, pp. 28, 29).

By trusting and believing God, not only is salvation real in our lives but, more importantly, we honor God in the vindication of His character to the world and universe. Most of us betray our inner sinfulness when we constantly pray "Lord, bless me and my loved ones, and don't forget me in thy kingdom. And bless the missionaries, evangelists, and pastors so the work can be finished and we can go home to glory."

Surely it is time to pray a more God-centered prayer of concern for the honor of Christ. We are pilgrims and strangers here on earth (Hebrews 11:13). May our prayers include proving the Father right in this great controversy between God and Satan. May we proclaim to the world as King David did, "O LORD, our Lord, how excellent is thy name in all the earth! who hast set thy glory above the heavens. Out of the mouth of babes and sucklings has thou ordained strength because of thine enemies, that thou mightest still the enemy and the avenger" (Psalm 8:1, 2).

God is on trial and we are His witnesses. "God forbid: yea, let God be true, but every man a liar; as it is written, That thou mightest be justified in thy sayings, and mightest overcome when thou art judged" (Romans 3:4). As we look toward heaven, we know that only those who are truthful will enter in: "And there shall in no wise enter into it any thing that defileth, neither whatsoever worketh abomination, or maketh a lie: but they which are written in the Lamb's book of life" (Revelation 21:27). May we defend Christ and the truth, because that is the only thing we can take to heaven. God has a remnant people that He will save; I pray each and everyone of us will be believers who will hasten, and not delay, Jesus' Second Coming.

Let us read some texts from two Old Testament authors, Ezekiel and King David, regarding the name of the Lord: and God's vindication.

"And I will sanctify my great name, which was profaned among the heathen, which ye have profaned in the midst of them; and the heathen shall know that I am the LORD, saith the Lord GOD, when I shall be sanctified in you before their eyes" (Ezekiel 36:23).

"He restoreth my soul: he leadeth me in the paths of righteousness for his name's sake" (Psalms 23:3).

Ellen White writes in *The Desire of Ages* about how we can honor God. "The honor of God, the honor of Christ, is involved in the perfection of the character of His people" (p. 671). By honoring God, we are helping to fight the great controversy. Ellen White speaks about the war we are waging:

"The fallen world is the battle-field for the greatest conflict the heavenly universe and earthly powers have ever witnessed. It was appointed as the theater on which would be fought out the grand struggle between good and evil, between heaven and hell. Every human being acts a part in this conflict. No one can stand on neutral ground. Men must either accept or reject the world's Redeemer. All are witnesses, either for or against Christ. Christ calls upon those who stand under His banner to engage in the conflict with Him as faithful soldiers, that they may inherit the crown of life. . . . The cross of Calvary challenges, and will finally vanquish, every earthly and hellish power. In the cross all influence centers, and from it all influence goes forth. It is the great center of attraction, for on it Christ gave up His life for the human race. This sacrifice was offered for the purpose of restoring man to his original perfection; yea, more. It was offered to give him an entire transformation of character, making him more than a conqueror. Those who in the strength of Christ overcome the great enemy of God and man, will occupy a position in heavenly courts above angels who have never fallen" (*Sons and Daughters of God*, p. 242).

If we are to reach others for Christ, our actions have to be like Jesus. "Our influence upon others depends not so much upon what we say as upon what we are. Men may combat and defy our logic, they may resist our appeals; but a life of disinterested love is an argument they cannot gainsay. A consistent life, characterized by the meekness of Christ, is a power in the world" (*The Desire of Ages*, p. 142).

By becoming like Jesus, we will finish the work and hasten the coming of Christ. "Christ is waiting with longing desire for the manifestation of Himself in His church. When the character of Christ shall be perfectly reproduced in His people, then He will come to claim them as His own" (Ellen G. White, *Christ's Object Lessons*, p. 69).

God's Word tells us that "the just shall live by faith: but if any man draw back, my soul shall have no pleasure in him. But we are not of them who draw back unto perdition; but of them that believe to the saving of the soul" (Hebrews 10:38, 39).

A great evangelist once said, "There are twelve inches between heaven and hell—the distance between the head and the heart."

May we believe in our heart God's Word to the saving of our soul. The previous scriptures and the Holy Spirit's insight are what brought about the fruit of trusting and believing God and experiencing righteousness by faith in our lives. I pray you will experience the same result to God's praise and His glory! Amen!

God Cannot Lie—Because He Said So!

Our trust and belief in God will grow if we remember that God's promises are true. He does not lie. We can rely on His Word for guidance and strength. Titus 1:1, 2 confirms the truth about God's trustworthiness: "Paul, a servant of God, and an apostle of Jesus Christ, according to the faith of God's elect, and the acknowledging of the truth which is after godliness; in hope of eternal life, which God, <u>that cannot lie</u>, promised before the world began."

"...these things saith the Amen, the faithful and true witness..." (Revelation 3: 14).

Learning From Children About Trusting God

A child believes in his heart that his mom and dad will take care of all his needs—food, clothing, shelter, and emergency care. Our heavenly Father can also supply all our needs since we are His sons and daughters, but we must trust Him like a little child trusts his parents. As we meditate on the words from our Lord's own lips, let us allow the Holy Spirit to lead us to a correct understanding of Scripture.

God promises us that as long as we seek after Him everything else will be taken care of: "Therefore I say unto you, take no thought for your life, what ye shall eat, or what ye shall drink; nor yet for your body, what ye shall put on . . . (For after all these things do the Gentiles seek:) for your heavenly Father knoweth that ye have need of all these things. But seek ye first the kingdom of God, and his righteousness; and all these things shall be added unto you" (Matthew 6:25-33).

Jesus affirmed the importance of having faith like a child: "Verily I say unto you, Whosoever shall not receive the kingdom of God as a little child, he shall not enter therein" (Mark 10:15).

When Enoch had his first child, he recognized this important fact and walked with God, and God was so pleased He took Enoch to heaven without seeing death. "And Enoch walked with God after He begat Methuselah three hundred years, and begat sons and daughters: And all the days of Enoch were three hundred sixty and five years: And Enoch walked with God: and he was not; for God took him" (Genesis 5:22-24).

What should be our attitude when studying God's Word?

"We must have the simplicity and faith of a little child, ready to learn, and beseeching the aid of the Holy Spirit. A sense of the power and wisdom of God, and of our inability to comprehend His greatness, should inspire us with humility, and we should open His word, as we would enter His presence, with holy awe. When we come to the Bible, reason must acknowledge an authority superior to itself, and heart and intellect must bow to the great I AM" (*Steps to Christ*, p. 110).

Righteousness by Faith

The Bible contains countless scriptures about faith and its development and importance in our lives. From a mathematical perspective, faith equals trusting and believing in God. Following are a number of verses that speak about faith and righteousness:

"For we through the Spirit wait for the hope of righteousness by faith" (Galatians 5:5).

"For what saith the scripture? Abraham believed God, and it was counted unto him for righteousness" (Romans 4:3).

"And being not weak in faith, he considered not his own body now dead, when he was about an hundred years old, neither yet the deadness of Sarah's womb: He staggered not at the promise of God through unbelief; but was strong in faith, giving glory to God; and being fully persuaded that, what he had promised, he was able to perform. And therefore it was imputed to him for righteousness" (Romans 4:19-22).

"Therefore being justified by faith, we have peace with God through our Lord Jesus Christ" (Romans 5:1).

"For unto us was the gospel preached, as well as unto them: but the word preached did not profit them, not being mixed with faith in them that heard it" (Hebrews 4:2).

"But without faith it is impossible to please him: for he that cometh to God must believe that he is, and that he is a rewarder of them that diligently seek him" (Hebrews 11:6).

What evaluation are we making of God if we do not have a living, child-like faith like Enoch and Abraham? John makes it clear in 1 John 5:10 the importance of believing in Christ: "He that believeth on the Son of God hath the witness in himself: he that believeth not God hath made him a liar, because he believeth not the record [the Bible] that God gave of his Son."

When we think about Christ's death and sacrifice for us, it focuses our minds on the truth and strengthens our faith. The following two texts confirm this thought: "I am crucified with Christ: nevertheless I live; yet not I, but Christ liveth in me: and the life which I now live in the flesh I live by the faith of the Son of God, who loved me, and gave himself for me" (Galatians 2:20), and "Always bearing about in the body the dying of the Lord Jesus, that the life also of Jesus might be made manifest in our body. For we which live are always delivered unto death for Jesus' sake, that the life also of Jesus might be made manifest in our mortal flesh" (2 Corinthians 4:10, 11).

Believing From the Heart

Not only must we focus our minds on Christ, but we must implant His Words into our hearts. "That if thou shalt confess with thy mouth the Lord Jesus and shalt believe in thine heart that God hath raised him from the dead, thou shalt be saved. For with the heart man believeth unto righteousness, and with the mouth confession is made unto salvation" (Romans 10:9, 10).

God's new covenant experience is putting His ten commandments on the tablets of our heart: "For this is the covenant that I will make with the house of Israel after those days, saith the Lord; I will put my laws into their mind, and write them in their hearts: and I will be to them a God, and they shall be to me a people" (Hebrews 8:10).

As we deepen our relationship with God, our love for Him will grow and we will love His commandments. "And this is love, that we walk after his commandments. This is the commandment, That, as ye have heard from the beginning, ye should walk in it" (2 John 1:6).

From reading the above scriptures, we can see that keeping the commandments is an act of love; pleasing God is where we find true happiness. The Bible and

Spirit of Prophecy continue additional evidence of this idea:

> "I delight to do thy will, O my God: yea, thy law is within my heart" (Psalms 40:8).

> "All who Love God will show that they bear His sign by keeping His commandments" (Ellen G. White, *Testimonies for the Church*, vol. 6, p. 265).

Lacking Faith and Obtaining More

So how do we obtain more faith if we are lacking it? God answers this question in His Word:

> "And all things, whatsoever ye shall ask in prayer, believing, ye shall receive" (Matthew 21:22).

> "So then faith cometh by hearing, and hearing by the word of God" (Romans 10:17).

For people who desire more faith to obey God's will in their lives, the secret is to pray sincerely and read God's Word. On a personal note, it was necessary for my wife and I to give our morning and evening daily devotional life top priority before we were able to see the Lord working in our lives.

Consider these verses:

"For whatsoever is born of God overcometh the world: and this is the victory that overcometh the world, even our faith" (1 John 5:4).

"Jesus said unto him, If thou canst believe, all things are possible to him that believeth" (Mark 9:23).

"As ye have therefore received Christ Jesus the Lord, so walk ye in him: Rooted and built up in him, and stablished in the faith, as ye have been taught, abounding therein with thanksgiving" (Colossians 2:6, 7).

God Loves Us—Because He Said So!

The Bible is clear about God's love for us. Isaiah 43:4 says, "You are precious in my eyes, and honored, and I love you" (RSV). "Yea, I have loved thee with an everlasting love" (Jeremiah 31:3).

Jesus came to save us from sin and reunite us with the Father! "For God so loved the world, that he gave his only begotten Son, that whosoever believeth in him should not perish, but have everlasting life" (John 3:16).

As the prophets foretold, the Messiah would come to redeem us: "And she shall bring forth a son, and thou shalt call his name JESUS: for he shall save his people *from their sins*" (Matthew1:21). Note: "Not *in* their sins"

Ellen White writes about why God sent His son to the earth:

"The whole purpose in giving His Son for the sins of the world is that man may be saved, not in transgression and unrighteousness, but in forsaking sin, washing his robes of character, and making them white in the blood of the Lamb. He proposes to remove from man the offensive thing that He hates, but man must co-operate with God in the work. Sin must be given up, hated, and the righteousness of Christ must be accepted by faith. Thus will the divine co-operate with the human. . . . He wants to restore His moral image to man (*Testimonies for the Church*, vol. 5, p. 632, 635).

Jesus' mission was "to bring to men complete restoration; He came to give them health and peace and perfection of character" (Ellen G. White, *The Ministry of Healing*, p. 17).

God is more than capable of saving us from our sins, but we must do our part and repent of our sins. "Behold, the LORD's hand is not shortened, that it cannot save; neither his ear heavy, that it cannot hear: But your iniquities have separated between you and your God, and your sins have hid his face from you, that he will not hear" (Isaiah 59:1, 2).

As Christians, God's Word tells us that if we have sin in our lives our prayers go no further than the ceiling. The only prayer God will hear is that of a heartfelt confession and repentance. (Read 1 John 1:9.) Only then can we tell Him of our concerns and needs. After that, God will give us power to continue our victorious walk with Jesus into His kingdom.

Because of God's love and His mercy toward us, we should be the happiest people in the world. King David wrote, "Bless the LORD, O my soul, and forget not all his benefits. He hath not dealt with us after our sins; nor rewarded us according to our iniquities" (Psalm 103:2, 10).

It certainly is good news that we don't have to suffer the penalty of the sins we have already committed. God wants us to benefit from the wonderful grace He has offered to us through Jesus' death on the cross. Praise God! Because of this gift, we don't have to experience the second death of being totally separated from God, and we don't have to miss out on living with God throughout eternity in heaven and the new earth. Following are a number of verses that speak about the promise of heaven and the joy that we will experience living with God forever:

"The wolf also shall dwell with the lamb, and the

leopard shall lie down with the kid; and the calf and the young lion and the fatling together; and a little child shall lead them" (Isaiah 11:6).

"And the inhabitant shall not say, I am sick: the people that dwell therein shall be forgiven their iniquity" (Isaiah 33:24).

"Then the eyes of the blind shall be opened, and the ears of the deaf shall be unstopped" (Isaiah 35:5).

"Violence shall no more be heard in thy land, wasting nor destruction within thy borders; but thou shalt call thy walls Salvation, and thy gates Praise" (Isaiah 60:18).

"And they shall build houses, and inhabit them; and they shall plant vineyards, and eat the fruit of them. They shall not build, and another inhabit; they shall not plant, and another eat: for as the days of a tree are the days of my people, and mine elect shall long enjoy the work of their hands" (Isaiah 65:21, 22).

"Nevertheless we, according to his promise, look for new heavens and a new earth, wherein dwelleth righteousness. Wherefore, beloved, seeing that ye look for such things, be diligent that ye may be found of him in peace, without spot, and blameless" (2 Peter 3:13, 14).

"And I John saw the holy city, new Jerusalem, coming down from God out of heaven, prepared as a bride adorned for her husband. And I heard a great voice out of heaven saying, Behold, the tabernacle of God is with men, and he will dwell with them, and they shall be his people, and God himself shall be with them, and be their God. And God shall wipe away all tears from their eyes; and there shall be no more death, neither sorrow, nor crying, neither shall there be any more pain: for the former things are passed away. . . . He that overcometh shall inherit all things; and I will be his God, and he shall be my son" (Revelation 21:2-4, 7).

In the new earth, sin will not arise a second time! We read this promise in Nahum 1:9: "What do ye imagine against the Lord? he will make an utter end: affliction shall not rise up the second time." There won't be sin again because on this side of the kingdom we are all being educated as to the character of Satan and the character of God. Our wonderful heavenly Father has proven Himself right in this great controversy; the love of God has won the battle. (Please read *The Desire of Age*, pp. 763-764.)

God promises that the new earth will be restored to

its original beauty. Isaiah wrote, "They shall not hurt nor destroy in all my holy mountain: for the earth shall be full of the knowledge of the LORD, as the waters cover the sea" (Isaiah 11:9). Also, in Revelation 22:3, it says, "And there shall be no more curse: but the throne of God and of the Lamb shall be in it, and his servants shall serve him" (Revelation 22:3).

God Forgives Us—Because He Said So!

We know that God forgives us because He says so! In 1 John 1:9, it says, "If we confess our sins, he is faithful and just to forgive us our sins, and to cleanse us from all unrighteousness."

King Solomon advises us against trying to cover our sins. Instead, if we repent of our sins, we will be covered by Jesus' blood. "He that covereth his sins shall not prosper: but whoso confesseth and forsaketh them shall have mercy" (Proverbs 28:13).

God Empowers Us—Because He Said So!

The same power that created the world in six days (Genesis 1; Psalms 33:6, 9 and 89:13-18), is the same power that gave Samson his super strength (Judges 14-16), healed the paralytic that had no use of his limbs for 38 years (Matthew 9:6), and gave victory to all of those witnesses who would have rather died than go against spiritual conscience (Hebrews 11). That same power can make us "overcomers" in Christ Jesus. (Read Revelations 2 and 3.)

Let us rejoice in the gospel of Christ: "For I am not ashamed of the gospel of Christ: for it is the power of God unto salvation to every one that believeth" (Romans 1:16). As we rejoice in God's gift, we will share our joy with others: "The gospel is to be presented, not as a lifeless theory, but as a living force to change the life. God desires that the receivers of His grace shall be witnesses to its power" (Ellen G. White, *The Desire of Ages*, p. 826).

God created this world by His spoken word and He empowers us to live a godly life. Hebrews 11:3 speaks about creation: "Through faith we understand that the worlds were framed by the word of God, so that things which are seen were not made of things which do appear" (Hebrews 11:3). King David also writes about creation and God's power: "By the word of the LORD were the heavens made; and all the host of them by the breath of his mouth. . . . For he spake, and it was done; he commanded, and it stood fast" (Psalm 33: 6, 9).

If we trust and believe in God, we not only believe we were created by God but that we can be re-created in Christ Jesus, experiencing the miracle of being born again: "Therefore if any man be in Christ, he is a new creature: old things are passed away; behold, all things are become new" (2 Corinthians 5:17).

So, can we all receive the power to keep sin out of our lives? John assures us that each one of us can be empowered by God. "But as many as received him, to them gave he power to become the sons [and daughters] of God, even to them that believe on his name" (John 1:12).

1 Corinthians 1:18 "For the preaching of the cross is to them that perish foolishness; but unto us which are saved it is the Power of God."

Calvary Conquered My Soul

Dear brethren, this is very important: when the cross of Christ becomes personal, we will, like Jesus, hate sin. It wasn't just the Jews or Roman soldiers 2000 years ago who crucified Christ; it was you and I.

The Bible states: "For he hath made him to be sin for us, who knew no sin; that we might be made the righteousness of God in him" (2 Corinthians 5:21). Isaiah foretold of Christ's sacrifice: "But he [Jesus] was wounded for our transgressions, he was bruised for our iniquities: the chastisement of our peace was upon him; and with his stripes we are healed" (Isaiah 53:5).

It is humbling to think that Christ bore our sins for us. In 1 Peter 2:24, 25, we read the following: "Who his own self bare our sins in his own body on the tree, that we, being dead to sins, should live unto righteousness: by whose stripes ye were healed. For ye were as sheep going astray; but are now returned unto the Shepherd and Bishop of your souls."

As we accept this gift, we cry out "create in me a clean heart, O God; and renew a right spirit within me" (Psalm 51:10). As we are transformed, we give up our heart for that of God's. "The sacrifices of God are a broken spirit: a broken and a contrite heart, O God, thou wilt not despise" (Psalms 51:17).

Once we have accepted Christ, we must remain strong in the faith lest we crucify Him again through our actions. "For it is impossible for those who were once enlightened, and have tasted of the heavenly gift, and were made partakers of the Holy Ghost, And have tasted the good word of God, and the powers of the world to come, If they shall fall away, to renew them again unto repentance; seeing they crucify to themselves the Son of God afresh, and put him to an open shame" (Hebrews 6:4-6).

In the tenth chapter of Hebrews, we find further counsel: "For if we sin willfully after that we have received the knowledge of the truth, there remaineth no more sacrifice for sins" (verse 26). If a non-believer hardens his heart against opportunities to accept Jesus, he will pay the penalty for his own sins—eternal death. (Read Isaiah 59:2 and Romans 6:23.) However, if a believer willfully sins against God, he is crucifying Christ anew.

I pray that God will forgive me and forgive you when we have fallen short. I want to, and I hope you want to, keep God's spiritual armor on that we may represent Christ to the world. May we love one another, live the abundant life, and, like Paul, "fight the good fight of faith" (1 Timothy 6:12). It's a good fight because we are on the winning side as long as we keep our eyes and heart focused on Jesus.

Let's continue our study by reviewing scriptures that speak about our victory in Jesus. We can overcome sin as long as we are in Jesus. He promises us that:

"For whatsoever is born of God overcometh the world: and this is the victory that overcometh the world, even our faith" (1 John 5:4).

"I can do all things through Christ which strengtheneth me" (Philippians 4:13).

"There hath no temptation taken you but such as is common to man: but God is faithful, who will not suffer you to be tempted above that ye are able, but will with the temptation also make a way of escape, that ye may be able to bear it" (1 Corinthians 10:13).

"Now unto him that is able to keep you from falling [sinning], and to present you faultless before the presence of his glory with exceeding joy" (Jude 1:24).

"I am crucified with Christ: nevertheless I live; yet not I, but Christ liveth in me: and the life which I now live in the flesh I live by the faith of the Son of God, who loved me, and gave himself for me" (Galatians 2:20).

"My sheep hear my voice, and I know them, and they follow me" (John 10:27).

Ellen White provides us the following insight into what led the disciples to follow Jesus:

"It is not the fear of punishment, or the hope of ever-lasting reward, that leads the disciples of Christ to follow Him. They behold the Saviour's matchless love, revealed throughout His pilgrimage on earth, from the manger of Bethlehem to Calvary's cross, and the sight of Him attracts, it softens and subdues the soul. Love awakens in the heart of the beholders. They hear His voice, and they follow Him" (*The Desire of Ages*, p. 480).

May we be strong in faith and obedience to God's will so that our example will help others to be strong. "The work of the Holy Spirit is to convince the world of sin, of righteousness, and of judgment. The world can only be warned by seeing those who believe the truth sanctified through the truth, acting upon high and holy principles, showing in a high, elevated sense, the line of demarcation between those who keep the commandments of God and those who trample them under their feet" (*S.D.A. Bible Commentary*, vol. 7, p. 980).

Ellen White wrote about the need for witnesses who can live a godly life. "The world needs a practical demonstration of what the grace of God can do in restoring to human beings the lost kingship, giving them mastery of themselves. There is nothing that the world needs so much as a knowledge of the gospel's saving power revealed in Christlike lives" (*The Ministry of Healing*, p. 132, 133).

Sharing Jesus with the world is our unique calling as Christians. "The very essence of the gospel is restoration, and the Saviour would have us bid the sick, the hopeless, and the afflicted take hold upon His strength" (Ellen G. White, *The Desire of Ages*, p. 824, 825). Our heavenly Father has called us to be ambassadors, sharing Christ with others (2 Corinthians 5:20). We can give Bible studies and literature to those who like to read, we can share CDs or audio tracks with those who like to listen, and we can lend videos to those who like to watch TV.

Remember, our actions speak louder than our words! We must be steadfast in our own relationship with God through prayer and Bible study in order to be a faithful witness for our Lord and Savior, Jesus Christ.

Ellen White writes, "The love of Christ, revealed to us, make us debtors to all who know Him not. God has given us light, not for ourselves alone, but to shed upon them. If the followers of Christ were awake to duty, there would be thousands where there is one today proclaiming the gospel in heathen lands. . . . We need not go to heathen lands, or even leave the narrow circle of the home, if it is there that our duty lies, in order to work for Christ. We can do this in the home circle, in the church, among those whom we associate, and with whom we do business" (*Steps to Christ*, p. 81)

Letting Our Light Shine

We have a great privilege and honor to glorify God by letting our light so shine that others can truly see Christ in us. "Let your light so shine before men, that they may see your good works, and glorify your Father which is in heaven" (Matthew 5:16).

No matter what we are doing, our end goal should be to glorify God: "Whether therefore ye eat, or drink, or whatsoever ye do, do all to the glory of God" (1 Corinthians 10:31).

Ellen White gives council to the church "There are many precious Truths contained in the Word of God, but it is "Present Truth" that the Flock needs now." Early Writings p. 63

"Let no soul complain of the servants of God who have come to them with a heaven-sent message. Do not any longer pick flaws in them, saying, 'They are too positive; they talk too strongly.' They may talk strongly; but is it not needed? . . . Satan has laid every measure possible that nothing shall come among us as a people to reprove and rebuke us, and exhort us to put away our errors. But there is a people who will bear the ark of God" (Ellen G. White, *Testimonies to Ministers and Gospel Workers,* pp. 410, 411).

Trusting and believing God will not only bring about revival but also reformation in our lives. We will think differently than the world, we will talk differently, and we will dress differently. We will no longer be in bondage to sin because Christ is living in our hearts. We all must make the choice between Christ or sin—we can't and don't want to have both.

Ellen White writes about the difference between revival and reformation: "A revival and a reformation must take place, under the ministration of the Holy Spirit. Revival and reformation are two different things. Revival signifies a renewal of spiritual life, a quickening of the powers of the mind and heart, a resurrection from spiritual death. Reformation signifies a reorganization, a change in ideas and theories, habits and practices. [Restoring God's ways in our lives and in our church.] Revival and reformation are to do their appointed work, and in doing this work they must blend" (*Selected Messages,* bk. 1, p. 128).

Let's take a closer look at the difference between revival and reformation. Revival is a renewal of our personal relationship with Jesus Christ, a re-dedication and a willingness to ask God for forgiveness and power by God's grace to surrender all to Jesus. On the other hand, reformation is from the root form, which means to make or create. "In the beginning God created the heaven and the earth. And God saw every thing that he had made, and, behold, it was very good" (Genesis 1:1, 31). But, then sin entered into the world and man was deformed. In order to bring man back to the original, he needed to be made new, hence the word reform or recreate. The suffix "ation" simply means "the process of." When we speak of a reformation, we speak of the process of bringing man back to his condition at creation, according to Peter Lausevic.

We must be reformed if we are to be ready for Christ's return. "Those who are to prepare the way for the second coming of Christ are represented by faithful Elijah, as John came in the spirit of Elijah to prepare the way for Christ's first advent. The great subject of reform is to be agitated, and the public mind is to be stirred. Temperance in all things is to be connected with the message, to turn the people of God from their idolatry, their gluttony, and their extravagance in dress and other things" (Ellen White, *Testimonies for the Church,* vol. 3, p. 62).

Ellen White provided a great deal of insight into Christian standards and the role we are to play in reaching others for Christ. Following is an excerpt from her book *Fundamentals of Christian Education*:

"As the truth is brought into practical life, the

standard is to be elevated higher and higher, to meet the requirements of the Bible. This will necessitate opposition to the fashions, customs, practices, and maxims of the world. Worldly influences, like the waves of the sea, beat against the followers of Christ to sweep them away from the true principles of the meekness and grace of Christ; but they are to stand as firm as a rock to principle. . . . We can stand firm only as our life is hid with Christ in God. . . . By conforming entirely to the will of God, we shall be placed upon vantage ground, and shall see the necessity of decided separation from the customs and practices of the world. We are not to elevate our standard just a little above the world's standard; but we are to make the line of demarcation decidedly apparent. . . . The reason we have had so little influence upon unbelieving relatives and associates is that we have manifested little decided difference in our practices from those of the world. . . . When we reach the standard that the Lord would have us reach, worldlings will regard Seventh-day Adventists as odd, singular, strait-laced extremists. . . . 'We are under solemn, sacred covenant to God to bring up our children, not for the world, not to put their hands into the hands of the world, but to love and fear God, and to keep His commandments" (pp. 288, 289).

According to Acts 3:19-21, Jesus will not return until God's ways are restored in His church—God's remnant people. "But Christ as a son over his own house; whose house are we, if we hold fast the confidence and the rejoicing of the hope firm unto the end" (Hebrews 3:6).

Ellen White once again calls God's people to repentance and a love for the truth in her book *Upward Look*:

> "The time has come when things must be called by their right names. The truth is to triumph gloriously, and those who have long been halting between two opinions must take their stand decidedly for or against the law of God. . . . The old truths are to be revived, in order that the false theories that have been brought in by the enemy may be intelligently met. There can be no unity between truth and error. We can unite with those who have been led into deception only when they are converted. There is a God, and I am commissioned to say that His truth must be vindicated, that the evil, seductive theories that are coming in may be uprooted. . . .
>
> "Once again, before the great destruction of the world by fire, there is granted a period of test and trial. Men are given opportunity to show whether or not they will be loyal to God. . . .
>
> "As God's witnesses, we have a message to

bear to all the world. The Lord has many children who have never heard the truth for this time. God's servants must give them the final warning" (*The Upward Look*, p. 88).

May we raise the standards back up in commandment keeping, health reform, reverence in the sanctuary, and dress reform. God did not change His mind regarding these practices and principles, which He shared with Ellen White. Furthermore, let's take the wedding ring back off in obedience to God's Word! (Read *Testimonies to Ministers and Gospel Workers*, p. 180, 181). (1 Timothy 2:9; 1 Peter 3:3,4)

"In the time of the end every divine institution is to be restored" (Ellen G. White, *Prophets and Kings*, p. 678). What were the divine institutions in the Garden of Eden? They were lifetime marriage commitment, Sabbath keeping, the original diet, and the plan of redemption. The Advent message in its fullness is designed to seal, or settle, a remnant people into living a total, heartfelt lifestyle in the image of Christ.

Let's read Isaiah 58:12: "And they that shall be of thee shall build the old waste places: thou shalt raise up the foundations of many generations; and thou shalt be called, The repairer of the breach, The restorer of the paths to dwell in." God will make everything whole again in His time.

Will we be ready? Are we willing to turn ourselves

over to God? Ellen White writes, "The word of God often comes in collision with man's hereditary and cultivated traits of character and his habits of life. But the good-ground hearer, in receiving the word, accepts all its conditions and requirements. His habits, customs, and practices are brought into submission to God's word. In his view the commands of finite, erring man sink into insignificance beside the word of the infinite God. With the whole heart, with undivided purpose, he is seeking the life eternal, and at the cost of loss, persecution, or death itself he will obey the truth" (Ellen G. White, *Christ's Object Lessons*, p. 60).

Each of us must account for our decisions. In relating to God's remnant people, there will be defective members. Worldliness and error will try to come in, but the church militant will fight against it to maintain the pillars of the faith and the truth of the gospel! (Please read *Selected Messages*, bk. 1, pp. 204, 205 and bk. 2, pp. 385, 390.)

We find in 1 Timothy 3:15 the call to hold fast to the truth. "But If I tarry long, that thou mayest know how thou oughtest to behave thyself in the house of God, which is the church of the living God, the pillar and ground of the truth."

In Ellen White's book *The Acts of the Apostles*, she writes about the church and its place in history, in the past and in the future:

"The church is God's fortress, His city of refuge, which He holds in a revolted world. Any betrayal of the church is treachery to Him who has bought mankind with the blood of His only-begotten Son. From the beginning, faithful souls have constituted the church on earth. In every age the Lord has had His watchmen, who have borne a faithful testimony to the generation in which they lived. These sentinels gave the message of warning; and when they were called to lay off their armor, others took up the work. God brought these witnesses into covenant relation with Himself, uniting the church on earth with the church in heaven. . . .

"Through centuries of persecution, conflict, and darkness, God has sustained His church. . . . His law is linked with His throne, and no power of evil can destroy it. Truth is inspired and guarded by God; and it will triumph over all opposition.

"During ages of spiritual darkness the church of God has been as a city set on a hill. From age to age, through successive generation, the pure doctrines of heaven have been unfolding within its borders. Enfeebled and defective as it may appear, the church is the one object which God bestows in a special sense His supreme regard" (pp. 11, 12).

Jesus pleaded in John 17 that His true followers would be as one. "And all mine are thine, and thine are mine; and I am glorified in them. And now I am no more in the world, but these are in the world, and I come to thee. Holy Father, keep through thine own name those whom thou hast given me, that they may be one, as we are" (John 17:10, 11).

We can trust Christ that the work He conducts in our life will be for His glory. "Being confident of this very thing, that he which hath begun a good work in you will perform it until the day of Jesus Christ. For to me to live is Christ, and to die is gain. Only let your conversation be as it becometh the gospel of Christ: that whether I come and see you, or else be absent, I may hear of your affairs, that ye stand fast in one spirit, with one mind striving together for the faith of the gospel" (Philippians 1:6, 21, 27).

The way we act, may it be to the glory of God. The way we talk, may it be to the glory of God. The way we eat, may it be to the glory of God. The way we dress, may it be to the glory of God. The way we resist tempta- tion, may it also be to the glory of God. The way we worship in God's sanctuary, may it be to the glory of God. "Offer unto God thanksgiving; and pay thy vows unto the most High: And call upon in me in the day of trouble: I will deliver thee, and thou shalt glorify me" (Psalm 50:14, 15).

When we resist temptation and do not sin, we glorify

the Father! If this is not our experience, how can it be
more of a reality in our lives? "Now the Lord is that
Spirit: and where the Spirit of the Lord is, there is liberty. But we all, with open face beholding as in a glass
the glory of the Lord, are changed into the same image
from glory to glory, even as by the Spirit of the Lord" (2
Corinthians 3:17, 18).

The *S.D.A. Bible Commentary* reminds us of the importance of looking toward Christ and following his example: "Beholding Christ means studying His life as
given in His Word. We are to dig for truth as for hidden
treasure. We are to fix our eyes upon Christ. When we
take Him as our personal Saviour, this gives us boldness
to approach the throne of grace. By beholding we become changed, morally assimilated to the One who is
perfect in character. By receiving His imputed righteousness, through the transforming power of the Holy Spirit,
we become like Him. The image of Christ is cherished,
and it captivates the whole being" (vol. 6, p. 1098).

We don't concentrate on our sins to get sin out of our
lives. We concentrate on Christ, and by beholding Him,
we are changed.

"Beloved, now are we the sons of God, and it doth
not yet appear what we shall be: but we know that, when
he shall appear, we shall be like him; for we shall see
him as he is" (1 John 3:2).

"Casting down imaginations, and every high thing
that exalteth itself against the knowledge of God, and
bringing into captivity every thought to the obedience of

Christ" we can overcome temptations and tribulations (2 Corinthians 10:5).

The Humanity of Christ

Let us consider the humanity of Christ that we may live the Christian life to the fullest. We are fortunate to have Jesus on our side, defending us in heaven since He was tested in all points that we are tempted (Hebrews 4:15).

Ellen White provides the following points regarding Jesus' humanity and how that relates to our experience on earth:

"If we had to bear anything which Jesus did not endure, then upon this point Satan would represent the power of God as insufficient for us. . . . He endured every trial to which we are subject" (*The Desire of Ages,* p. 24).

"Jesus revealed no qualities, and exercised no powers, that men may not have through faith in Him. His perfect humanity is that which all His followers may possess, if they will be in subjection to God as He was" (Ibid, p. 664).

"The obedience of Christ to His Father was the same obedience that is required of man. . . . He came not to our world to give the obedience of a lesser God to a greater, but as a man to obey God's holy law, and in this way He is our example. The Lord Jesus came to our world, not to reveal what a God could do, but what a man could do, through faith in God's power to help in every emergency" (*S.D.A. Bible Commentary*, vol. 7, p. 929).

The secret of success to living a godly life is to put on the mind of Christ and have the faith of Jesus! "Forasmuch then as Christ hath suffered for us in the flesh, arm yourselves likewise with the same mind: for he that hath suffered in the flesh hath ceased from sin; That he no longer should live the rest of his time in the flesh to the lusts of men, but to the will of God" (1 Peter 4:1, 2). In Philippians 2:5, we are urged to "let this mind be in you, which was also in Christ Jesus."

As we look to Christ, he will strengthen us and we will become His witnesses: "Here is the patience of the saints: here are they that keep the commandments of God, and have the faith of Jesus" (Revelation 14:12).

Once we are risen with Christ, we will "seek those things which are above, where Christ sitteth on the right hand of God. Set your affection on things above, not on things on the earth" (Colossians 3:1, 2).

If there is any worldliness in our lives or in our church, in the name of Jesus, may we obey God's clear instruction. My reason for bringing the following things to your attention is not to condemn anyone but to restore, if possible, God's glory that the church militant can become the church triumphant. Let us be open to following counsel as King Solomon advises us to do: "He is in the way of life that keepeth instruction: but he that refuseth reproof erreth." (Proverbs 10:17)

As we shun the world, the world will know that we follow God. "They are of the world: therefore speak they of the world, and the world heareth them. We are of God: he that knoweth God heareth us; he that is not of God heareth not us. Hereby know we the spirit of truth, and the spirit of error" (1 John 4:5, 6).

Let us make sure we do not conform to the world: "And be not conformed to this world: but be ye transformed by the renewing of your mind, that ye may prove what is that good, and acceptable, and perfect, will of God" (Romans 12:2).

As we set ourselves apart from the world, I recommend that you study the following areas and passages from the Bible and Spirit of Prophecy:

• Worldly beauty, (dress, makeup, jewlery, etc.) versus God's beauty. (Deuteronomy 22:5; 1 Timothy 2:9; 1 Peter 3:3, 4; and *Testimonies for the Church*, vol. 1, p. 461 and vol. 5, p. 96)

• Worldly eating habits versus God's original diet. (*Counsels on Diet and Foods,* p. 380, 381; and *Testimonies for the Church*, vol. 2, p. 352, 373, 374) (Genesis 1:29; 3:18) (1 Corinthians 9:25) Nuts, grains, fruits, and vegetables eaten temperately!

• Worldly psychology versus God's Word. (Proverbs 3:5, 6 and 14:12; Matthew 4:4; and Acts 5:29)

• Sports, hobbies, TV jobs, etc. If we get consumed in them and have no time to study God's Word, they become our gods. Be careful! Lets not break Commandment #1. (Exodus 20:3 amd Romans 13:14)

Should we be worried about the current state of Christianity and the church? Ellen White warns us against succumbing to the world: "The minds of many have been so darkened and confused by worldly customs, worldly practices, and worldly influences that all power to discriminate between light and darkness, truth and error, seems destroyed" (*Testimonies for the Church*, vol. 5, p. 62)

In the book *Spiritual Gifts*, Ellen White warns again about the power of Satan: "The power of Satan now to tempt and deceive is ten-fold greater than it was in the days of the apostles" (vol. 2, p. 277). In order to fight against Satan, we must become more like Jesus: "Christianity means perfect conformity to the Christ-life" ("Be Ye Therefore Perfect," *The Signs of the Times*, July 17, 1901).

Testing Ourselves, Are We Genuine Christians?

How can we test ourselves to see if we are genuine Christians who trust and believe in God? Look at the following scriptures and see if you are measuring up to Christ's standards.

Love is the greatest test!

"My Little children, let us not love in word, neither in tongue; but in deed and in truth." (1 John 3:18).

May we all read the love chapter in 1 Corinthians 13 often to keep love supreme in our lives.

"Beloved, let us love one another for love is of God; and everyone that loveth is born of God; and knoweth God."

"For to this end also did I write, that I might know the proof of you, whether ye be obedient in all things" (2 Corinthians 2:9).

"Wherefore by their fruits ye shall know them. Not every one that saith unto me, Lord, Lord, [Christian, Christian] shall enter into the kingdom of heaven; but he that doeth the will of my Father which is in heaven" (Matthew 7:20, 21).

". . . the fruit of the spirit is love, joy, peace, long
suffering, gentleness, goodness, faith. Meekness,
tempered: against such there is no law."
(Galations 5:22m 23)

"If we live in the Spirit, let us also walk in the
Spirit. (Galations 5:25).

"Husbands, love your own wives, even as Christ
also loved the church, and gave himself for it."

"Wives, submit yourselves unto your own husbands, as unto the Lord. For the husband is the
head of the wife, even as Christ is the head of the
Church, and he is the savior of the body."
(Ephesians 5:25, 22, 23)

"If any man will come after me, let him deny
himself, and take up his cross, and follow me"
(Matthew 16:24).

Faith Versus Presumption

So what is the difference between faith and presumption? Consider these words from Ellen White: "Only he
who has true faith is secure against presumption. For
presumption is Satan's counterfeit of faith. Faith claims
God's promises, and brings forth fruit in obedience.
Presumption also claims the promises, but uses them as

Satan did, to excuse transgression. Faith would have led our first parents to trust the love God, and to obey His commands. Presumption led them to transgress His law, believing that His great love would save them from the consequence of their sin. It is not faith that claims the favor of Heaven without complying with the conditions on which mercy is to be granted. Genuine faith has its foundation in the promises and provisions of the Scriptures." (*The Desire of Ages,* p. 126-127).

Ellen White offers additional counsel to God's people regarding our place in the world:

"We cannot be half the Lord's and half the world's. We are not God's people unless we are such entirely. . . . The church cannot measure herself by the world nor by the opinion of men nor by what she once was. Her faith and her position in the world as they now are must be compared with what they would have been if her course had been continually onward and upward. The church will be weighed in the balances of the sanctuary. If her moral character and spiritual state do not correspond with the benefits and blessings God has conferred upon her, she will be found wanting" (*Testimonies for the Church,* vol. 5, p. 83).

Character Decides Our Destiny

"Then said Jesus to those Jews which believed on him, If <u>ye continue in my word, then are ye my disciples indeed</u>; And ye shall know the truth, and the truth shall make you free. They answered him, We be Abraham's seed, and were never in bondage to any man: how sayest thou, Ye shall be made free? Jesus answered them, Verily, verily, I say unto you, <u>Whosoever committeth sin is the servant of sin</u>. And the servant abideth not in the house forever: but the Son abideth ever. If the Son therefore shall make you free, ye shall be free indeed. <u>I know that ye are Abraham's seed; but ye seek to kill me</u>, because my word hath no place in you. I speak that which I have seen with my Father: and ye do that which ye have seen with your father. They answered and said unto him, Abraham is our father. <u>Jesus saith unto them, If ye were Abraham's children, ye would do the works of Abraham. But now ye seek to kill me</u>, a man that hath told you the truth, which I have heard of God: this did not Abraham. <u>Ye do the deeds of your father</u>. Then said they to him, We be not born of fornication; we have one Father, even God. <u>Jesus said</u> unto them, <u>If God were your Father, ye would love me</u>: for I proceeded forth and came from God; neither came I of myself, but he sent me. Why do ye not understand my speech? even because ye cannot hear my word. <u>Ye are of your father the devil, and the lusts of your father ye will do</u>. He was a murderer from the beginning, and abode not in the truth, because there is no truth in him. When he speaketh a lie, he speaketh of his own: for he is a liar, and the father of it" (John 8:31-44).

"Not every one that saith unto me, Lord, Lord, (Christian, Christian) shall enter into the kingdom of heaven; but he that doeth the will of my Father which is in heaven" (Matt 7:21).

> Our Salvation is not based on going to Church and calling ourselves Christians! Being a Christian will give us entrance to God's Kingdom. Lord help me to be Faithful.

God does not lie! He is committed to saving us:

"So shall my word be that goeth forth out of my mouth: it shall not return unto me void, but it shall accomplish that which I please, and it shall prosper in the thing whereto I sent it" (Isaiah 55:11).

Dear brethren, have you allowed God's Word to accomplish what it pleases in you? Are you bringing every thought into conformity to the Word? Have you allowed the Word to change your desires, your tastes in eating and drinking and dressing? What about your speech? Have you experienced victory over anger, impatience, and gossip? When you rise each morning and kneel by your bed, do you, by faith, take up your cross and follow the meek and lowly Jesus? May we not compromise our standards for that of the world. Daniel, Shadrach, Meshach, and Abednego had that type of character.

For your encouragement, take a moment and read just what kind of character these four Hebrew men had:

> "But Daniel purposed in his heart that he would not defile himself with the portion of the king's meat, nor with the wine which he drank: therefore he requested of the prince of the eunuchs that he might not defile himself" (Daniel 1:8).

> "Nebuchadnezzar spake and said unto them, Is it true, O Shadrach, Meshach, and Abednego, do not ye serve my gods, nor worship the golden image which I have set up? Now if ye be ready that at what time ye hear the sound of the cornet, flute, harp, sackbut, psaltery, and dulcimer, and all kinds of musick, ye fall down and worship the image which I have made; well: but if ye worship not, ye shall be cast the same hour into the

midst of a burning fiery furnace; and who is that God that shall deliver you out of my hands?

"Shadrach, Meshach, and Abednego, answered and said to the king, O Nebuchadnezzar, we are not careful to answer thee in this matter. If it be so, our God whom we serve is able to deliver us from the burning fiery furnace, and he will deliver us out of thine hand, O king. But if not, be it known unto thee, O king, that we will not serve thy gods, nor worship the golden image which thou hast set up.

"Then Nebuchadnezzar spake, and said, Blessed be the God of Shadrach, Meshach, and Abednego, who hath sent his angel, and delivered his servants that trusted in him, and have changed the king's word, and yielded their bodies, that they might not serve nor worship any god, except their own God" (Daniel 3:14-18, 28).

The three Hebrews would not break the commandments of God even if it meant death to them! May we have that same devotion.

To find others of equal faith, read Job 1:1; Luke 1:5,6; Hebrews 11th chapter, and Rev. 14:12. These are God's Faithful remnant in these last days hastening Jesus Second Coming!

Now is the Time for Preparation

"I saw that many were neglecting the preparation so needful and were looking to the time of 'refreshing' and the 'latter rain' to fit them to stand in the day of the Lord and to live in His sight. Oh, how many I saw in the time of trouble without a shelter! They had neglected the needful preparation; therefore they could not receive the refreshing that all must have to fit them to live in the sight of a holy God. Those who refuse to be hewed by the prophets and fail to purify their souls in obeying the whole truth, and who are willing to believe that their condition is far better than it really is, will come up to the time of the falling of the plagues, and then see that they needed to be hewed and squared for the building. But there will be no time then to do it and no Mediator to plead their cause before the Father" (Ellen G. White, *Early Writings*, p. 71). (Read also *Testimonies to Ministers and Gospel Workers*, p. 16, 17.)

No matter what happens, we must hold firm to the Savior and keep looking toward heaven. Read Jeremiah 12:5: "If thou hast run with the footmen, and they have wearied thee, then how canst thou contend with horses? and if in the land of peace, wherein thou trustedst, they wearied thee, then how wilt thou do in the swelling of Jordan?" If we are having problems with the footmen (small compromises or temptations), then what are we going to do with the horses and the swelling of the Jordan (National Sunday Law, etc.)?

We must not compromise our stand. We must put our trust and belief in God and strengthen our faith now. Otherwise, like Peter, who didn't feel his need to watch and pray, we will fall when the big temptations and tests comes.

Which of the following examples can you relate with?

- I and Christ are one, and I am the *one*. (A carnal believer; read 1 Corinthians 3:1-3; Galatians 5:19-21; Romans 8:6.)

- I and Christ are one, and He (Christ) is the *One*! (A spiritual believer; read Philippians 4:13; Galatians 2:20; 1 John 4:4.)

As Christians we want Jesus in the drivers seat. Do we tell Him how to drive or let Him do the driving?

Who Shall Have Salvation?

King David questioned, "Lord, who shall abide in thy tabernacle? who shall dwell in thy holy hill? He that walketh uprightly, and worketh righteousness, and speaketh the truth in his heart" (Psalm 15:1, 2). If we repent of our sins and have faith in Jesus, we shall be saved (Acts 20:21).

Let's take a closer look at what God's Word says

about grace and what it will accomplish in the believer's life.

> "For the grace of God that bringeth salvation hath appeared to all men, teaching us that, denying ungodliness and worldly lusts, we should live soberly, righteously, and godly in this present world, looking for that blessed hope, and the glorious appearing of the great God and our Saviour Jesus Christ" (Titus 2:11-13).

> "And as it is appointed unto men once to die, but after this the judgment: So Christ was once offered to bear the sins of many; and unto them that look for him shall he appear the second time without sin unto salvation" (Hebrews 9:27, 28).

> "And every man that hath this hope in him purifieth himself; even as he is pure" (1 John 3:3).

> "Let integrity and uprightness preserve me; for I wait on thee" (Psalm 25:21).

The Reality of The Second Coming of Christ

With all the trials and disappointments that exist in everyday life, the closest thing to my heart is the reality of the blessed hope of Jesus' Second Coming. The Bible teaches that if we stay focused on Jesus, the devil can't steal that hope from us.

Ellen White wrote, "We believe without a doubt that Christ is soon coming. This is not a fable to us; it is a reality. . . . When He comes He is not to cleanse us of our sins, to remove from us the defects in our characters, or to cure us of the infirmities of our tempers and dispositions. If wrought for us at all, this work will all be accomplished before that time. When the Lord comes, those who are holy will be holy still. Those who have preserved their bodies and spirits in holiness, in sanctification and honor, will then receive the finishing touch of immortality. But those who are unjust, unsanctified, and filthy will remain so forever. No work will then be done for them to remove their defects and give them holy characters. . . . Many of us are rough stones from the quarry. But as we lay hold upon the truth of God, its influence affects us. It elevates us and removes from us every imperfection and sin of whatever nature" (*Testimonies for the Church*, vol. 2, p. 355).

An Appeal to God's People

For the past 25 years, I have been a member of the Seventh-day Adventist Church and have been told that Jesus' Second Coming is very near. Why hasn't Jesus come back yet?

Let me say it another way, can we now pray at this

time—please come Lord Jesus! Or Lord don't come just
yet, I know I'm not ready!

Let's look at 2 Peter 3:9 and 12 for our answer: "The
Lord is not slack concerning his promise, as some men
count slackness; but is longsuffering to us-ward, not
willing that any should perish, but that all should come
to repentance. Looking for and hasting unto the coming
of the day of God."

"And now little children, abide in him, that, when he
shall appear, we may have confidence, and not be
ashamed before him at his coming." (1 John 2:28)

Dear Brother, how would we be ashamed? "Having
a form of godliness, but denying the power thereof . . ."
(2 Timothy 3:5) I believe the scripture teaches that
known sin still in our lives would make us feel ashamed.

"Be patient therefore, brethren, unto the coming of
the Lord. Behold, the husbandman waiteth for the precious fruit of the earth, and hath long patience for it"
(James 5:7).

Our wonderful heavenly Father gave us His best
when Jesus became the Savior of the world.After reading the Bible from Genesis to Revelation, I get the im-
pression that God wants to save us more than we want to
be saved. Time is running out; probation ends at death or
Jesus' Second Coming. (Read Revelation 22:7, 11-14).

Let nothing get in the way of spending eternity with
God in heaven and the new earth. No sin is worth giving

up God's precious promise. Read Ellen White's counsel about living our lives for Christ as she wrote in *The Adventist Home*:

> "If you have become estranged and have failed to be Bible Christians, be converted; for the character you bear in probationary time will be the character you will have at the coming of Christ. If you would be a saint in heaven, you must first be a saint on earth. The traits of character you cherish in life will not be changed by death or by the resurrection. You will come up from the grave with the same disposition you manifested in your home and in society. Jesus does not change the character at His coming. The work of transformation must be done now. Our daily lives are determining our destiny." p. 16

We cannot change our character but Jesus can. His mission on earth was not only to die for our sins but to transform our character to be more like Christ, acceptable to the Father. We must trust and believe God from the heart!

We have been told by Ellen White that Jesus could have come the second time after the Great Disappointment in 1844 if they would have held fast their faith, receiving the Third Angel's Message and in the power of the Holy Spirit proclaiming it to the world. (Read *Se-*

lected Messages, vol. 1, pp. 68-69.) Jesus could have also come in 1888 if the church would have accepted the message of righteousness by faith by E.J. Waggoner and A.T. Jones. (Read *Testimonies to Ministers and Gospel Workers*, pp. 90-93.)

(I recommend the following books: *Christ and His Righteousness* by E.J. Waggoner and *Christ Our Righteousness* by Athur G. Daniels.)

Ellen White offers the following advise as to the delay in Christ's coming and how we can serve Him until His return:

"The long night of gloom is trying; but the morning is deferred in mercy, because if the Master should come, so many would be found unready. God's unwillingness to have His people perish has been the reason for so long delay" (Testimonies for the Church, vol. 2, p. 194).

"I know that if the people of God had preserved a living connection with Him [Jesus], if they had obeyed His Word, they would today be in the heavenly Canaan" (*The General Conference Bulletin*, March 30, 1903).

"It is the privilege of every Christian, not only to look for, but to hasten the coming of our Lord Jesus Christ. Were all who profess His name bearing fruit to His glory, how quickly the whole world would be sown with the seed of the gospel. Quickly the last harvest would be ripened, and Christ would come to gather the precious grain" (*Testimonies for the Church*, vol. 8, p. 22).

We must continue to trust in the Lord and wait upon Him, making sure that we are the wheat and not the tares. In Matthew 13:25-30, Jesus spoke to the people about the wheat and the tares growing together until the harvest. They were both members of the church, but only God's faithful remnant (the wheat) were gathered into the barn of eternal life.

In Zephaniah 13:12 and 13, the prophet speaks about God's remnant: "I will also leave in the midst of thee an afflicted and poor people, and they shall trust in the name of the LORD. The remnant of Israel shall not do iniquity, nor speak lies; neither shall a deceitful tongue be found in their mouth: for they shall feed and lie down, and none shall make them afraid."

The Church Militant is Becoming the Church Triumphant

Ellen White chronicles her first vision in the book *Early Writings*, which showed God's people traveling along a narrow path. "While I was praying at the family altar, the Holy Ghost fell upon me, and I seemed to be rising higher and higher, far above the dark world. I turned to look for the Advent People in the world, but could not find them, when a voice said to me, 'Look again, and look a little higher.' At this I raised my eyes, and saw a straight and narrow path, cast up high above the world. On this path the Advent people were traveling to the city, which was at the farther end of the path. They had a bright light set up behind them at the beginning of the path, which the angel told me was the midnight cry. This light shone all along the path and gave light for their feet so that they might not stumble. If they keep their eyes fixed on Jesus, who was just before them, leading them to the city, they were safe. . . .

"Soon we heard the voice of God like many waters, which gave us the day and hour of Jesus' coming. The living saints, 144,000 in number, knew and understood the voice, while the wicked thought it was thunder and an earthquake. . . . The 144,000 were all sealed and perfectly united. On their foreheads was written, God, New Jerusalem, and a glorious star containing Jesus' new name" (pp. 14, 15).

"It was at midnight that God chose to deliver His people. . . . Soon appeared the great white cloud, upon which sat the Son of man. When it first appeared in the distance, this cloud looked very small. The angel said that it was the sign of the Son of man. As it drew nearer the earth, we could behold the excellent glory and majesty of Jesus as He rode forth to conquer. . . . He did not wear a crown of thorns, but a crown of glory rested upon His holy brow.

Upon His vesture and thigh was a name written, King of kings, and Lord of lords" (pp. 285, 286).

We are awaiting the time when Jesus will stand up for His people and call them to Him. "The seal of the living God is upon His. people. This small remnant, unable to defend themselves in the deadly conflict with the powers of earth that are marshaled by the dragon host, make God their defense" (*Testimonies for the Church,* vol. 5, pp. 212, 213).

Christ loves His church and gave Himself for it "that he might sanctify and cleanse it with the washing of water by the word, that he might present it to himself a glorious church, not having spot, or wrinkle, or any such thing: but that it should be holy and without blemish" (Ephesians 5:25-27).

The following questions are posed in scripture for our contemplation:

"For the great day of his wrath is come; and who shall be able to stand?" (Revelation 6:17).

"Who shall ascend into the hill of the LORD? or who shall stand in his holy place? He that hath clean hands, and a pure heart; who hath not lifted up his soul unto vanity, nor sworn deceitfully" (Psalm 24:3, 4).

Of course, God knows our thoughts. "Search me, O

God, and know my heart: try me, and know my thoughts: And see if there be any wicked way in me, and lead me in the way everlasting" (Psalm 139:23, 24).

As we near Christ's return, let us be joyful and love one another with an everlasting love. "Let us be glad and rejoice, and give honour to him: for the marriage of the Lamb is come, and his wife hath made herself ready." Also, in 1 John 4:12 and 17, we read, "No man hath seen God at any time. If we love one another, God dwelleth in us, and his love is perfected in us. Herein is our love made perfect, that we may have boldness in the day of judgment: because as he is, so are we in this world."

Yes, God's remnant church, His "noble ship" (*Selected Messages*, bk. 2, p. 390), will be ready because they have learned to appreciate salvation and have also learned to trust and believe God through righteousness by faith.

It is our hope and prayer that through this study with the aid of the Holy Spirit you may believe God and truly experience the miracle of being born again, which is the early rain. As you mature, you will prepare for the latter rain at which time the church militant may become the church triumphant.

As we near the close of this study, I want to leave you with a variety of Bible verses that speak about our responsibility as Christians and God's promises to us:

"Open ye the gates, that the righteous nation

which keepeth the truth may enter in. Thou wilt keep him in perfect peace, whose mind is stayed on thee: because he trusteth in thee. Trust ye in the LORD for ever: for in the LORD JEHOVAH is everlasting strength" (Isaiah 26:2-4).

"And I will give them an heart to know me, that I am the LORD: and they shall be my people, and I will be their God: for they shall return unto me with their whole heart" (Jeremiah 24:7).

By God's Grace and Power may the Lord's Prayer be a reality in our own lives. "After this manner therefore pray ye: Our Father which art in heaven hallowed be thy name. Thy kingdom come. Thy will be done in earth, as it is in heaven" (Matthew 6:9, 10).

May our minds, hearts, and eyes be focused on God's Kingdom. "But seek ye first the kingdom of God and his righteousness . . ." (Matthew 6:33).

"But be ye doers of the word, and not hearers only, deceiving your own selves" (James 1:22).

"The LORD bless thee, and keep thee: The LORD make his face shine upon thee, and be gracious unto thee: The LORD lift up his countenance upon thee, and give thee peace" (Numbers 6: 24-26).

"He which testifieth these things saith, Surely I come quickly. Amen. Even so, come, Lord Jesus. The grace of our Lord Jesus Christ be with you all. Amen" (Revelation 22:20, 21).

In Christian love for the Brethren
Rick M. Streight

Closing Thoughts

Following are a few closing thoughts that are of utmost importance. After the brief thought, I have included a scripture or scriptures that relate to the key point.

1. Compared to eternity with God, this life here on earth is so short, God's Word calls it a vapor.

   "Whereas ye know not what shall be on the morrow, for what is your life? It is even a vapour, that appeareth for a little time, and then vanisheth away" (James 4:14) Read also (1 Peter 1:24 & Ecclesiastes 1:4 and verse 11).

   We prepare ourselves for this temporary world by learning a job so we can make a living. It makes even more perfect sense to prepare for eternity with God! If we have neglected reading the Bible to know God's will for us, we have good advice from scripture: "Seeing then that ye walk circumspectly (watchful) not as fools, but as wise, Redeeming the time because the days are evil" (Ephesians 5:15, 16).

   "And Philip said, If thou believeth with all thine heart, thou mayest [be baptized]. And he answered and said, I believe that Jesus Christ is the Son of God" (Acts 8:37).

2. It is not faith and works, it is faith that works.

    Read John 14:15 and Revelation 22:7, 11-14.

3. "Whosoever is born of God doth not commit sin; for his seed remaineth in him: and he cannot sin, because he is born of God" (1 John 3:9).

    "If we say that we have no sin, we deceive ourselves, and the truth is not in us" (1 John 1:8).

    These scriptures seem to contradict each other, but not so! It is unknown sin in our lives that keeps us from saying we are sinless. (Read Job 34:31, 32; John 9:41; and Acts 17:30)

4. With man this is possible.

    To learn about Jesus, Be Baptized, and join the S.D.A. Church.

    With God all things are possible.

    Not only join the Church but have a Born again Experience of putting on The Mind of Christ & having The Faith of Jesus. (Philippians 2:5; Revelation 14:12)

5. In the Parable of the Ten Virgins (Matthew 25:1-

13), take notice that the wise virgins were also asleep while the bridegroom (Jesus) tarried (verse 5).

"And that, knowing the time, that now it is high time to <u>awake out of sleep</u>: for now is our salvation nearer than when we believed." (Romans 13:11)

We must [wake up] and "Prepare to meet thy God . . ." (Amos 4:12)

6. Relating to the importance of character maturity E.G. White says . . . "Not one of us will ever receive the seal of God while our characters have one spot or stain upon them. It is left with us to remedy the defects of our characters, to cleanse the soul temple of every defilement. Then the latter rain will fall upon us as the early rain fell upon the disciples on the day of Pentecost." Testimonies to the Church Volume 5, page 214

7. Salvation or God's Vindication: Which comes first? An additional quote from the Servant of the Lord, E. G. White, should answer this question clearly!

"But the plan of redemption had a yet broader and deeper purpose than the salvation of man. It was not for this alone that Christ came to the earth; it was not merely that the inhabitants of this little world might regard the law of God as it should be regarded; but it was to <u>vindicate the character of God before the universe</u>....The act of Christ in dying for the salvation of man would not only make heaven accessible to men, but before all the universe, it would justify God and his Son in their dealing with the rebellion of Satan." (*Patriarchs and Prophets*, pp. 68, 69)

The Great Controversy between God and Satan must be settled once and for all before Jesus' Second Coming can be a reality! We, as God's remnant people, have been given that responsibility. Read (Luke 12:32) and (4 *BC* 1161)

8. At the 59th Seventh-day Adventist General Conference session, our new president, Ted Wilson, preached on <u>Going Forward</u> not Backwards. [Revival and Reformation was the thrilling catchword.]

Pray for our worldwide church. May we talk more about what <u>we can do</u> in Christ Jesus and <u>less on what we can't do in our own fallen nature</u>.

Other Available Studies

1. *In Defense of the King James Bible*
2. *Principles in God's Word to Come to a Correct Understanding of Truth*

"My sheep hear my voice, and I know them, and they follow me" (John 10:27)

"They are not of the world, even as I am not of this world. Sanctify them through thy truth: thy word is truth. . . . That they all may be one; as thou, Father, art in me, and I in thee, that they also may be one in us: that the world may believe that thou hast sent me" (John 17:16, 17, 21).

The conclusion of the whole matter is that <u>we are the church</u>—"a called out and be ye separate people." We are not like the world. We are different. We are Christians.

(Comments or questions welcome)

Address: Rick M. Streight
      703 Shirley Drive
      Aberdeen, MD 21001

      Phone: (410)272-0728
      E-mail: rockmanrick@live.com

We invite you to view the complete
selection of titles we publish at:

www.TEACHServices.com

or write or email us your praises,
reactions, or thoughts about this
or any other book we publish at:

TEACH Services, Inc.
P.O. Box 954
Ringgold, GA 30736

info@TEACHServices.com

Finally, if you are interested in seeing
your own book in print, please contact us at

publishing@teachservices.com.

We would be happy to review your manuscript for free.

www.ingramcontent.com/pod-product-compliance
Lightning Source LLC
Chambersburg PA
CBHW060441090426
42733CB00011B/2353